Hope and the Sea

poems by
Magda Portal

for Tano & Ayelet —
with love,

Kathleen ~ 06/19/2021

Translated from the Spanish by
Kathleen Weaver

Dulzorada Press

HOPE AND THE SEA

© 2021, Dulzorada Press
Editor-in-chief: José Garay Boszeta
Email: jose@dulzorada.com
Cover design and layout: Miguel Garay Boszeta
Email: miguel@dulzorada.com
Dulzorada logo design: Bidkar Yapo @nacion.chicha

ISBN-13: 978-1-953377-03-6 (paperback)
ISBN-13: 978-1-953377-04-3 (hardcover)
Published by Dulzorada Press
http://Dulzorada.com

Printed in the USA

CONTENTS

Translator's Preface

Born May 27, 1900, in the seaside resort town of Barranco, Magda Portal (María Magdalena Julia Portal Moreno) experienced a comfortable, even idyllic early childhood, the second of four Portal children. To further his successful construction business, her father relocated the family to the port town of Callao, acquiring a large, rambling house near the ocean, a house replete with ghost stories that delighted the children. These easeful days ended sadly with the death of Pedro Portal from a brief, feverish illness. His young widow, Rosa Amelia, was left the task of sorting out the obscure tangle of his business affairs. Following failed legal battles, as properties and personal possessions were sold to pay debts, only the great house remained. Unscrupulous machinations led to their loss of that important asset, and Magda as a child of seven found herself standing in the street, forcibly evicted with her siblings, sobbing, banging on a padlocked door. This experience, she believed, predisposed her from then on to identify with society's ill-treated and dispossessed.

Rosa Amelia found work as a seamstress, eventually remarried, and had five additional children. When Magda was seventeen her stepfather died, leaving the family again without means, now in Lima. Having acquired secretarial skills, Magda, along with her elder sister, worked to help support the large household. With no money to attend university, one day she dared enter the campus and sit in on a class at the University of San Marcos, her first step into the world of Lima's dissident students and activists. In that ambiance she became a friend of Peru's great poet César Vallejo, who introduced her to "deep Peru," the world of Peru's impoverished indigenous majority. Peru was then in the throes of a rapidly modernizing, destabilizing social change. The Mexican and Russian Revolutions were recent events, inspiring what became known as a "vanguard generation" in Peru. Strikes, campesino rebellions, and student agitations were underway.

As a girl Magda wrote prolifically, reams of poetry, short stories, sentimental novels, efforts she often destroyed, although she shared a good deal of her writing, which her mother encouraged. In the early 1920s her poems began appearing in Lima's literary journals. It was in those circles that she met the Bolaños brothers —Federico, Reynaldo, and Oscar, who would figure so decisively in her life. Of indigenous heritage, the attractive brothers were vitally interested in literature and politics. The younger brothers took on pseudonyms, becoming known as Serafín Delmar, and Julián Petrovick. Magda was especially drawn to Federico, the eldest, also a poet, and they became a couple. In 1923 she became pregnant with his child, with no intention of marrying him, an unconventional behavior that appalled and estranged her mother, a traditional Catholic. But Magda stubbornly refused to conform. The couple retreated to the Andean town of Huancayo where the brothers had been raised.

All along she worked on poetry, submitting (under the pseudonym Lorelei) a winning selection to Lima's most prestigious literary contest, *Los Juegos Florales* (The Floral Games). In August 1923, at the elegant awards ceremony attended by Lima's social and literary elite, she waited in the wings, dressed in a lovely evening gown. When she realized that Peru's autocrat, Augusto B. Leguía, had entered the auditorium—a figure despised by young dissidents—she refused to go on stage to recite her poems. Her repudiation of the strongman became notorious. Yet how astonishing it still seems to me that—so very visibly pregnant and unmarried—she was invited to recite her poems on stage. Her situation, absolutely contrary to prevailing mores, was somehow tolerated in this instance.

A few months later, on November 23, 1923, a daughter was born in Lima, Gloria, and Magda returned with the infant to live with Federico in Huancayo. By 1924 Magda and the three Bolaños brothers were publishing the first vanguardist literary magazine in Peru, *Flechas* (Arrows), which folded after six issues. The contents reveal a bombastic eagerness to insult a society they deemed moribund and worthy only of being swept away.

In July of that year Magda and Federico were sacramentally married, ending the unsustainable estrangement from her beloved mother. By this time, however, their relationship was very likely under great strain. Federico was said to be jealous, patriarchal, even physically abusive —hardly a suitable match for the free-spirited young woman. The connection failed, and at some point Magda became involved with her husband's brother, Serafín Delmar, also a gifted writer. Late in 1925, Magda, with Serafín, and her daughter, left Peru for Bolivia, leaving behind a very difficult situation.

Serafín Delmar: the pseudonym may be translated seraph of the sea, which adds a further sense to Magda's poems of yearning to be at one with the ocean. Magda's half-sister Graciela described Serafín as "the great love" of her sister's life. Tall, slender, with green eyes and dark hair with a shock of white, he presented a very handsome figure. Of a milder, more circumspect nature than his elder brother, his temperament appears to have been very compatible with Magda's need for freedom and independence. In the high-altitude city of La Paz, the two participated in student marches and agitprop protests against Bolivia's strongman. They contributed to incendiary student magazines and published a joint collection of prose poems, provocatively titled *El Derecho de Matar* (The Right to Kill), activities that led to their deportation late in 1926, escorted across the border by Bolivian police.

Again in Lima, they found their way into the Amauta circle, the group assembled around the brilliant Marxist intellectual and labor leader, José Carlos Mariátegui. *Amauta*, his legendary journal of art and social thought, was the most influential of that era in Latin America, a journal cosmopolitan in scope, leftist in orientation, and open to the indigenous world. Mariátegui was the teacher of those who gathered in his cordial living room in the late afternoons: writers, painters, anthropologists, sociologists, traveling journalists, often with labor leaders coming and going. The gatherings were informal, convivial, people sitting wherever they could in a room overflowing with books and magazines from abroad. All sorts of ideas were under discussion, including the urgency of transforming Peru, a society in rapid flux but still grounded in semi-feudal social relations. A hereditary landed elite owned vast tracts of land, while indigenous people were exploited in debt peonage on great plantations.

In the course of a formative European sojourn in the early 1920s, Mariátegui traveled widely, absorbing intellectual and political currents, including the ideas of Marx, George Sorel, and other social theorists. Mariátegui embraced Marxism in a non-doctrinaire fashion, with the aim of applying its methods to Latin American social conditions. Shortly after his return to Lima with his Italian wife, Ana de Chiappe, Mariátegui became ill with a bone cancer that led to the loss of one leg and the disability of the other. Confined to a wheelchair, he resumed, even intensified, his writing, publishing, and labor-organizing activities, aware he might not have long to live. Mariátegui's radiant kindness and superior mind made him not only greatly respected but also very much loved by his friends and followers.

Magda sympathized with radical ideas concerning social justice but described herself in those days as "barely a poet," and only beginning to be exposed to social thought. Seated on the floor near Mariátegui's wheelchair, she listened intently. At one point Magda placed a sheaf of her poems in Mariátegui's hands. Early in 1927, the Minerva Press published *Una esperanza y el mar* (Hope and the Sea), as well as a volume of poems by Serafín Delmar, *Radiogramas del Pacífico* (Radiograms of the Pacific).

Composed in the "vanguardist" style, under the influence of futurism, dada, surrealism, these are companion volumes in which each poet acknowledges a love for the other. A further collection of Magda's poems was announced as forthcoming from the Minerva Press.

This must have been an especially happy and invigorating episode in the lives of Magda and Serafín, each of them now with books in print, which significantly raised their literary profiles. Their poems often appeared in *Amauta*, and on festive excursions with Mariátegui and other writers, they read their poems to factory workers on Lima's outskirts. A new magazine devoted to labor was in the works, while the gatherings at Mariátegui's house continued.

But all this came to a stark end when, on June 10, 1927, Peru's strongman ordered a sweep of arrests. Hundreds of activists were jailed, including Mariátegui in his wheelchair. Left-wing projects, including the journal *Amauta* and the Minerva Press, were shut down for an extended period.

A day or so after these arrests, Magda was utterly stunned to be summoned to a Lima police department and told she was being deported, immediately. Days later she and her daughter, along with Serafín and other political deportees, were put on a ship headed for Havana. After weeks in Cuba the Peruvians went on to Mexico City, where the future schism in Peru's left began to emerge in exile. The deported Peruvians readily accepted the tutelage of the charismatic Peruvian student leader Víctor Raúl Haya de la Torre, expelled from Peru a few years earlier. They became part of his inner circle and key players in Haya's APRA movement: American Popular Revolutionary Alliance —a revolutionary nationalist tendency with an internationalist Pan-American vision. This nascent and very ambitious movement offered itself as an alternative to the communist movement in Latin America. Eventually it would have a presence in many countries. What a tumult of left wing debates in Mexico City. Diego Rivera and Frida Kahlo were part of the fast-moving political and artistic scene. It was a heady moment for the young Peruvians.

As months passed in intense political discussions "under the Mexican stars," Haya de la Torre announced that Magda's poetry presented an obstacle to her political formation. He wanted her to quit poetry and study political economy. Magda agreed, and in Mexico City in 1928, standing on a bridge over a stream, she ripped up an early manuscript, dropping scraps into the water as her friends looked on in astonishment. She would not write poetry, she declared, until she understood the meaning of imperialism in Latin America. Even as she was destroying her manuscript, she later explained, she knew she was not abandoning poetry forever. It was her way of announcing that she had made a commitment.

Following a whirlwind and historic speaking tour in the Caribbean in 1929, Magda awaited the opportunity to return, along with other Peruvian exiles. Finally, in 1931, the strongman deposed, the exiles began coming home. But Mariátegui was no longer there, having died at age thirty-five before they were able to meet with him in Chile and possibly resolve their political differences. So it was that Haya's revolutionary nationalist approach, as opposed to a more Soviet-oriented socialism, went forward with intense momentum, and Magda became a co-founder of the APRA Party of Peru, and a tireless leader of its women's organization.

APRA, the first mass party in Peru's history, was built from the ground up in a frenzy of organizing, extending for the first time into Peru's rugged, indigenous highlands —with the aim of winning a national election. Had the APRA won, it would have taken power as the first democratically-elected revolutionary government in Latin America. But APRA lost, barely, and the country was plunged into years of political instability and violence, a tumult typical of Peru's undemocratic history. Factions in APRA went on to foment insurrections, even assassinations, one of which was said to have been plotted in the home of Magda and Serafín. In 1932, Serafín was arrested, and Magda was forced into hiding for many months. Serafín would be tried, convicted, and imprisoned in a harsh penitentiary in Lima for a hard, saddening ten years. His younger brother, Julián Petrovick, also suffered prison as an APRA militant. Magda too would be arrested and jailed, in 1934, with no charges filed. She served nearly five hundred days in prison. Once freed, she would leave Peru, traveling and giving talks in Bolivia, Uruguay, Argentina, and other countries, finally settling for an extended exile in Chile. All the while her daughter remained with her.

In Peru or in exile Magda encouraged women to better themselves and become leaders in the civil and political arena, as well as in their own families, working as equal partners with men to achieve social redress, recognizing that women needed to confront men on issues of domination, but at that same time unite with men to confront the grotesquely unfair distributions of wealth. Above all she promoted education, urging women to take initiative in every realm, challenging them to defeat the tyrant within themselves, "the ignorance, the indolence, the conformity . . . ." As women they would need to fight for every gain. "No one will do it for us," she declared. She also promoted women's collectives and practical projects to help women develop their abilities. Her fame and influence in the 1930s and 1940s in a number of Latin America countries, especially Peru, cannot be overstated. Her audacious and indefatigable efforts have led to her being recognized as a pioneering figure in the history of Latin American social struggles, a champion of women and of the poor, as well as a writer with a significant body of work, not only in poetry. She produced an important autobiographical novel, with a theme of political betrayal and disillusion, *La Trampa* (The Trap), as well as essays and journalistic and political writings.

In his seminal work, *Seven Interpretive Essays on Peruvian Reality*, Mariátegui praised Magda for the honesty and tenderness of her sensibility. He described her as "Peru's first woman poet." Other Peruvian women were accomplished as poets, he acknowledged, but in Magda's poetry he discerned a new voice, a deeply-felt expression of woman's entire being, one embracing the eros of having a body and experiencing sexual passion.

Her poems in this collection often arise from an irrepressible need to cry out under the pressure of intimate experience, the inebriation of desire, the anguish of simply waiting, or of being relentlessly watched, or being subject to painfully constricting forces. A yearning for freedom is a principal motif, and it is personal, even to the extent of her wanting to be free of her very self—the intensity of experience may be almost too much to bear.

Her desire for liberation extends to all who are oppressed, exploited, displaced, all "who bear their hearts in their open hands." The current of sadness running throughout her poetry is intrinsic to her sensibility, a feeling akin to Christian apprehension of sacrificial lives. Human suffering may darken the spectacle but the poet's fierce belief in life itself, in the need to endure suffering and to resist injustice—that faith, that hope for humanity, is never abandoned. "Hope alights on the waves / white seagull / with dawn-colored eyes."

Above all, *Hope and the Sea* is a work exquisitely youthful in spirit —desirous, exhilarated, libertarian in its vivacity and volatility. The poems express a radical openness to experience, in which anguish intermingles with the thrill of modernity, of first voyages, new inventions, new loves. A presiding image is that of the sea, ever-beckoning toward far horizons, emblematic of great adventure and vaulting dreams.

Hope and the Sea may foreshadow a moment when poetic reverie would need to be suppressed, postponed by a disciplined political will, but that moment was not yet. Never again would a volume of Magda Portal's poems convey such a sense of unbridled possibility, the future so open, the kaleidoscopic display of states of mind so intoxicatingly engaging.

As Magda's remarkable life unfolded, she endured a number of severe blows. When reunited with Serafín Delmar in Chile, after a decade of his being jailed, a betrayal of trust on Serafín's part brought their long love affair to a bitter end. Despite his repeated apologies and fervent appeals for reconciliation, Magda would not relent.

A short while later, back in Peru in 1947, Gloria Delmar, her daughter, committed violent suicide in the family home. Magda's friends and political comrades feared she would not survive the unspeakable shock and grief. At the same time the APRA Party was veering hard right, abandoning the radical social agenda, even to the point that leader Haya de la Torre proclaimed that women could no longer be full members of the

16

party. Instead, after decades of sacrifice, deaths, and serious activism on the part of thousands of Aprista women in the organization led by Magda Portal, women were demoted to being merely adjunct members. Magda objected in outraged protest. In 1950, under house arrest under another oppressive Peruvian strongman, she denounced, in specific detail, the party she had co-founded, and in so doing found herself ostracized and her life threatened. Supported by a small cadre of like-minded party members, she withdrew for a time from public life, emerging to devote herself to a dynamic schedule of writing, cultural activities, and further political concerns, in a long, indomitably active life. The rise of the women's movement in the 1970s brought her historic activism to the attention of a new generation, and Magda embraced the new movement with alacrity.

In the 1930s she refused to identify with the suffragettes, seeing in the single issue of the vote the narrow attitude of a privileged class of Peruvian women. This polemical stance would give way to a full embrace of women's efforts to attain equality in all realms. In 1944 in Chile, she described the women's revolution as the most transcendent of all time, one being accomplished over millennia and without major bloodshed. By the 1970s she identified happily with the word feminist, placing her hope in the young and in the future.

This 1927 volume was my introduction to Magda Portal's poetry, the key to my later researching her life, about which I knew nothing when I first read these poems with an eye to extracting anthology pieces, as the co-editor of *The Penguin Book of Women Poets* in the 1970s. This targeted approach can hurry one past far too many poems, which together constitute the poetic vision. How much more rewarding to linger, poem by translated poem, with no option of ignoring a poem I didn't quite understand, or if it seemed my translation didn't work. As translator I've tried to trace the language to its source in a mind, in experience. But what does that mean when it comes to conveying a poem's subjectively perceived impression and aura, how to keep faith with that task? A moment comes when I'm uncertain how to proceed, wondering if one or another liberty or interpretative departure is a misstep. In any case, it's a privilege to have been able to translate, with the invaluable assistance of José Garay Boszeta, —and with that of Rocío Revolledo Pareja— my favorite collection by Magda Portal, my esteemed and dear late friend.

We first met in person in early June 1981, in Berkeley. After attending a women's conference in Mexico City, she visited Daniel Reedy in Lexington, then traveled on to San Francisco to spend time with Zoila Maxwell, her friend and former comrade in the APRA, whose family sheltered her at great risk when she was living in hiding in Peru. For many days Magda was available for activities, and I was able to interview her at length. The dizzying array of episodes she narrated became the impetus for my biographical study with translations, *Peruvian Rebel, The World of Magda Portal*. At that point she was no longer the woman who had written these early poems. "I've survived myself," she said, in a moment of sudden reflection in our interview, and yet somehow she was that woman. Her spirited and thoroughly charming presence at age eighty-one seemed to affirm the existence of that "continuous and permanent self" in which, as Katherine Mansfield observed, we persist in believing.

K.W., Berkeley, March 19, 2021

Hope and the Sea

—Lima, 1927—

VARIOS POEMAS

A LA

MISMA DISTANCIA

VARIOUS POEMS
AT THE
SAME DISTANCE

FRENTE A LA VIDA

Frente a la Vida
recojo este grito desgarrado
ancha ola que se estrella en
la playa de mi corazón

NO TENGO PROCEDENCIA

amo la Tierra
porque vengo del seno de la Tierra
pero tengo los brazos
          tendidos al mar

el sol castiga mis espaldas
y la sonrisa de la mañana
tiene besos salobres

abre sus rejas la ciudad
para los esclavos del hambre
donde el hombre tatuado de tristeza
muerde el pan cuotidiano:

"todos los días son iguales"

gran argolla
          ojos de ajusticiado
manos que arañan las ideas oscuras
nubes alegres
          alegría del campo
             alegría del cielo
                alegría del mar

FACING LIFE

Facing Life
I take up this unbridled cry
broad wave crashing on
my heart's beach

I HAVE NO PRECEDENT

I love the Land
because I come from its bosom
but my arms
                    reach toward the sea

the sun beats on my shoulders
morning's smile
has brackish kisses

the city opens its iron gates
to let in hunger's slaves
where man   tattooed with sadness
gnaws his daily bread:

"every day is the same"

heavy shackle
                    eyes of an executed man
hands scratching at obscure ideas
light-hearted clouds
                    joy of the fields
                        joy of the sky
                            joy of the sea

A L E G R Í A   vidrios rotos   las lágrimas
quiebran en arcoíris el paisaje

persignado de amor
                con la pequeña cruz a cuestas
hombre esclavo   pequeño hijo de la Tierra
donde todo es prestado
                hasta la luz que ríe
sobre su frente condenada

encarcelado hombre de ayer
hierve el mar subterráneo del pasado
donde se nutren las raíces
                de los hombres de hoy

amarrados al recuerdo
                espectros detrás de nuestras pisadas
como la tara de la sangre

siempre somos los hijos
        d e   l o s   p a d r e s

con la garra que muerde nuestros talones
de la carne   de la patria   de dios

Pero Yo   Yo
                frente a la vida
yo poseo la roja manzana de la Vida
y estoy aquí   enorme Mar
                humano Mar
                Mar mío

HAPPINESS   shattered windows   teardrops
blur the landscape's rainbow

signed by the cross of love
                a small cross on his back
enslaved worker   humble son of the Earth
where everything's on loan
                even the light laughing down
on his condemned forehead

jailed man of yesterday
the subterranean sea of the past boils
where the roots of today's men
                draw nourishment

chained to memory
                specter tracking our steps
like blood guilt

always we are
        o u r   p a r e n t s '   c h i l d r e n

talon of flesh   of fatherland   of god
biting at our heels

But I   I
            facing Life
I hold in my hand its red apple
and I am here   enormous sea
        human Sea
        my Sea

tú   el único libre bajo el cielo
tú que azotas las nubes
          con banderas de espuma que enrojece el crepúsculo
tú que me has enseñado
                la alegre tristeza del viaje

HOMBRE EMIGRANTE

    recién HOMBRE LIBRE

        NO TENGO PROCEDENCIA

alarido del Mar
detrás de las colinas azules
el Sol compañero de todos los días
me saluda en el don de la mañana
y la ancha ola
hunde en la playa de mi corazón
sus rojos dedos libertarios

you   the only free thing under the sun
you lash the clouds
        with flags of sunset-reddened foam
you have taught me
           the joyful sadness of the journey

IMMIGRANT MAN

    newly liberated   MAN

        I HAVE NO PRECEDENT

yell of the Sea
behind blue hills
the Sun companion of every day
greets me with the gift of morning
and the broad wave
sinks in the beach of my heart
its libertarian crimsons

CANTO PROLETARIO

"la vida es de los felices"
amanece en todos los pregones callejeros
rueda la mañana sobre el asfalto de
la tierra ululante y caliente

al extremo de la ciudad
los árboles saludan al obrero
con sus ramas estremecidas
por la alegría del viento vagabundo
                    el gran libertario

Como un dolor sigue la sombra
la silueta del hombre
que desemboca en la ancha
puerta de la fábrica
allí   el humano acecido de las máquinas
el gemido de las poleas
bajo la presión del pensamiento humano

balcones a la eternidad
los ojos siguen la labor constructora
y toda la fábrica es una sola
maquinaria de empuje formidable
como un titánico organismo
que mueve "el motor maravilloso"
de los cerebros de 100 hombres unidos
el hermoso espectáculo del cerebro
y el músculo en acción
el sudor les decora la cara

PROLETARIAN SONG

"Life belongs to the lucky"
dawns in the street vendors' cries
morning wheels over the asphalt
of screeching hot earth

trees at the city outskirts
salute the worker
with branches tossed
by the gaiety of vagabond wind
              the great libertarian

Like pain a shadow tracks
the silhouette of a man
entering the wide
factory gates
in the interior   men panting over machines
the groan of pulleys
under the weight of human thought

balconies onto eternity
eyes follow the constructive labor
the entire factory a single mechanism
a titanic organism
of formidable thrust
powered by "the marvelous motor"
of the brains of 100 united men
the beautiful spectacle of mind
and muscle in action
sweat decorates their faces

como otra sonrisa
que se tuesta en los labios apretados
de anhelo
la fábrica lo es todo

            la ESPERANZA y la CARCEL

Todos los días son MAÑANA
para el obrero que los lleva apretados
al corazón
            como la imagen de la madre

LIBERTAD
            estandarte del hombre

el Sol espera la salida de la fábrica
desde el horizonte sus anchos brazos de luz
saludan el dolor del obrero
            vencedor de la Vida

like a kind of smile
burning on lips
tense with concentration
the factory is everything

THE HOPE   THE PRISON

Every day is TOMORROW
for the worker who takes them
to heart
          like a mother's picture

LIBERTY
          raised ensign of man

the Sun waits at the factory exit
broad arms of horizon-light
salute the pain of the worker
                    conqueror of Life

11

el gran ruido del mar estrellándose en las paredes
de mi cráneo
en cuyos frontales golpea la idea
de la más libre libertad
para extender mis manos afiladas y firmes
a los muros cerrados de la muerte

alegre capacidad de los sentidos
para desamarrarse de las costas del amor
y salir sobre los mares desconocidos
a los puertos sin nombre

N O C H E
      círculo de mis pensamientos
donde dan vueltas desesperadas las mariposas neurasténicas

ruidos indiferentes
para aunándose al estrépito con que golpean las
paredes de mi cráneo
          todos los ruidos
A l e g r í a
      la de mis dos pupilas
ventanas a una casa de locos
la de mis recuerdos de antes
apiñados en las astas de mis sentidos
como pájaros sobre postes eléctricos
y mis brazos
      afilados y firmes
tendidos hasta tocar las paredes de piedra
de la muerte

11

the great roar of the sea crashing against the
plates of my skull
in whose frontal lobes
the idea of utter freedom strikes
my honed determined hands
reach toward the sealed door of death

happy capacity of the senses
unmoored from the shores of love
to venture on unknown seas
toward nameless ports

NIGHT
        closed circuit of my thoughts
where neurasthenic butterflies
wheel desperately

indifferent sounds
add to the awful racket in my brain
                        battering noises
Gaiety
        that of my two pupils
windows in the madhouse
of my memories from before
crowded on the masts of my senses
like birds on high voltage wires
and my arms
        honed and determined
reach out and touch
death's stone barricade

12

mi soledad aguaita
las esquinas vacías de la Noche

aquí estoy apretada
en las paredes del silencio

la duda me hace signos
desde el alféizar de su sonrisa

gatos neurasténicos pasean
en los tejados del recuerdo
las lucecitas de sus ojos
como automóviles de cita

¡oh CIUDAD!
          cuando te agarrarán
los remolinos de mis ojos
para que te hundas definitivamente

creo en el arcoíris de la alegría
en los mil faroles eléctricos
que decoran la catedral de tu cuerpo

honda que arroja piedras a los pájaros
juventud cazadora de emociones
pero allí está la FUERZA
sobre los rieles del deseo

12

my loneliness keeps watch
in the night

deserted street corners
walls of silence press me

doubt beckons
from the windowsill of its smile

along rooftops of memory
neurotic cats parade
the tiny headlights of their eyes
like cars where lovers meet

oh CITY!
        when will the
whirlpools of my eyes
seize and engulf you absolutely

I believe in rainbow happiness
in the thousand electric light bulbs
decorating the cathedral of your body

sling hurling stones at birds
youth   stalker of emotions
but this is   FORCE
hurtling along rails of desire

allá
  las torres más altas
lucen reclamos para los habitantes
de los otros planetas

in the distance
                        skyscrapers
beam advertisements to the inhabitants
of other planets

PACIFIC STEAM

recién noche vientre negro de fiera amaestrada
tus pasillos se encienden con luciérnagas de sueño

arrinconada está la flor de mis veinte años
como una niña de cabellos largos

mar del color del jersey de la mañana
balanceo embriagante
sin palabras   armonía de lo silencioso

cortando el transatlántico el presente
enarboladas manos de adiós
          gritaban las gaviotas
pañuelos inútiles   sin respuesta

el rojo capitán obeso y el japonés
de ojos tatuados de deseo
flechas tiradas al azar   las siluetas de las
pasajeras
          la pianola es un grito destemplado
el corazón del mar abrazado de oscuridad

viajeras pálidas   ojos anestesiantes
hombres que fuman cigarrillos de recuerdo

por las claraboyas de la noche
se asomó la mañana

EN SUS MANOS TRAÍA LA COSTA

PACIFIC STEAM

nightfall black womb of a domesticated animal
your corridors spark with dream fireflies

cornered flower of my twenty years
like a girl with streaming hair

sea the color of morning's blouse
intoxicating roll of the waves
speechless   harmony of the silent

steamship cleaving the present
hands unfurl goodbyes
       seagulls shriek
handkerchieves wave   with no reply

the obese red captain   and the Japanese
with desire-tattooed eyes
haphazard arrows   silhouettes
of passengers
       the pianola is a dissonant wail
the sea's heart flooded with darkness

pale women   anesthetizing eyes
men inhaling memories like nicotine

through the skylights of the night
morning shone

BEARING THE COAST IN ITS HANDS

39

13

AMISTAD   eje cercado de distancias
polo norte a donde llega el Sol cada seis meses
todos tus osos blancos gruñen hermosamente

yo soy salvajemente h e r m a n a
como los vientos cálidos que soplan de los trópicos
para envolver en sus anillos
las ciudades dispersas del globo

intercontinental   cosmopolita y amargamente huraña
mis ojos lentes zeiss de ultrapotencia
impresionan múltiple y cósmica la Vida

AMISTAD   terciopelo de lujurias suaves
vanidad de chiffones
expresión de mujer del siglo XIX

yo soy como los yodos y las sales del mar
de vastedad jadeante   donde recién se sabe el
vértigo
ASÍ
          donde todo es posible

Todas las naves emisarias de la alegría
inflan sus velas en mis vientos

para no asirme a nada
abrí los brazos en el signo más amplio
también el mar tiene los brazos abiertos

13

FRIENDSHIP   axis circled by distances
north pole where every six months the Sun arrives
all your white bears growl beautifully

I am savagely s i s t e r
like the warm winds swirling out of the Tropics
to envelop in their rings
the scattered cities of the globe

intercontinental   cosmopolitan and bitterly shy
my eyes   ultra-powerful Zeiss lenses
register multiple and cosmic life

FRIENDSHIP   plush velvet of luxuries
vanity of chiffons
expression of the nineteenth century woman

I am like the salts and iodines of the sea's
gasping immensity   just now I
know vertigo
THUS
      where all is possible

All the ships emissaries of happiness
fill their sails with my winds

to be tied to nothing
I opened my arms in the broadest sign
the sea too has open arms

mentira sus sirenas de encanto
los hombres no aman el mar
sino los caminos del mar

por eso yo que nunca fui mendiga
devuelvo lo que absorben los remolinos de mis ojos
impregnado del radio de mis cavernas cerebrales

Y como el mar   surcada de veleros en viaje hacia
los puertos del Futuro
            sin gaviotas de amor   trayectoria de soles en
el sistema de la Vida
esta noche que la luna echa sus anclas en mi indiferencia

            m e   s i e n t o   s o l a

A M I S T A D
            todas las distancias tienden sus paralelas
al infinito para no tocarse jamás

LOS ÁNGULOS SON H E R M A N O S

its sirens of enchantment all are lies
men do not love the sea
but the paths across it

That is why I could never beg
I give back what the whirlpool of my eyes absorbs
transmitting the radio waves of my humming brain

Like the sea   furrowed by ships
steaming toward Future ports
          with no seagulls of love   trajectory of suns in
Life's galaxy
tonight when the moon drops its anchor in my indifference

      I   f e e l   a l o n e

F R I E N D S H I P
          when all the distances extend their parallels
to infinity so as not to touch

ANGLES ARE B R O T H E R S

POEMA

fumando mi cigarro de spleen
quiebro la frágil humarada del recuerdo
el caracol del mar adormece mis nervios

todas mis costas están bañadas con la
sal de tus besos

mi voluntad lleva sus transatlánticos
hacia la China
pasando por la esclusa
que abrió en la entraña de la tierra
el deseo de los hombres

paisaje color de té
los amarillos descubrieron que eran hombres
con farolillos de papel encendiendo kilómetros

de pie en las astas de la vida
guardo un equilibrio imposible

trepidante alegría
locomotora sin frenos   mis nervios
fósforos encendidos   se derriten sobre
los dos abismos claros

horizonte bordado de esperanzas
sin dibujar

mañana reventarán los cohetes de mi dolor
incendiando los cien pisos del presente

POEM

smoking my cigarette of spleen
I break the fragile haze of recollection
the spiral shell of the sea lulls my nerves

all my coasts are bathed with
your salt kisses

my will propels its steamers
toward China
passing through floodgates
dug through the heart of earth
by the desire of men

landscape the color of tea
yellow races discover their humanity
with paper lanterns kindling kilometers

upright on the mast of life
I keep an impossible balance

trembling euphoria
locomotive without brakes   my nerves
lit matches   stream over
two transparent chasms

horizon embellished by
nebulous hopes

tomorrow the rockets of my pain will explode
and set on fire the hundred-storeyed present

IMAGEN

Kms superpuestos cabalgando las distancias
todos los trenes partían sin llevarse mi
anhelo viajero

        y al otro lado

me estaría esperando yo misma
con los brazos en las astas del tiempo

Ciudades con los nervios de acero
aguardando los muelles de mis ojos
para embarcar emigrantes   que
se llevan el corazón en las manos
para que picoteen las gaviotas
de la ausencia

Yo quiero las ciudades donde
el hambre de los H O M B R E S
se ha trepado por los rascacielos
y se enreda a los radiogramas
del espacio

      para llorar su esclavitud
Ciudades congestionadas de epilepsia
donde nos damos con la
                muerte
                   a la
vuelta de cualquier esquina

IMAGE

Superimposed kilometers astride distances
Train after train departing without taking
my yearning to travel

        and on the other side

I would be awaiting myself
with my arms on the rigs of time

Steel-nerved cities
await the landing docks of my eyes
to receive the immigrants
who hold their hearts in their open hands
for the seagulls of absence
to pick apart

I want cities where
humanity's H U N G E R
has scaled the tallest buildings
to mingle with the radiograms
of space

      to lament its captivity
Convulsive cities where
at every turn we come up against
                    death

Yo quiero
                    pero en vano
en vano se alargan mis ojos como
grúas en la distancia profunda
que no miden sino Kms   Kms

        detrás de cuyas murallas
están las ciudades que sueño

I desire
                  but in vain
in vain my eyes reach like
construction cranes into the furthest distance
            kilometers   kilometers

        beyond whose walls are
the cities I dream

14

en el cristal del agua
cortaron los paisajes su alegría
y todas las estrellas
lloraron lágrimas de luz

mañana emigrarán los pájaros
al más lejano mapa
los trenes tiran su modorra
y echan su gran serpiente
a caminar sobre las pampas doradas

    ¡los trenes!
ahora que está lejos el mar

Yo resuelvo el problema de mi angustia
con el boleto del pasaje

Allá   cómo se expande al infinito
el horizonte
cada mañana llega con su equipaje de esperanza
que resulta vacío
anochece
en el cinema de mis ojos
ya no se filman más paisajes

14

in the glassy water
landscapes curtail their happiness
all the stars
blink tears of light

tomorrow birds will migrate
to the furthest map
trains will shake off their stupor
and launch their tremendous serpent
on shimmering yellow plains

      —the trains!
already the sea is far behind

I solve the problem of my anguish
with a railway ticket

In the distance   how the horizon
expands into infinity
each day arrives with its baggage of hope
which turns out to be empty
night falls
the cinema of my eyes
films no more landscapes

15

la luna de aumento de la mañana
ha duplicado el paisaje matemático
ahora todo tiene un doble porcentaje de Sol

mi cuerpo fino de mujer civilizada
arrebujado en brumas neurasténicas
se desnuda a la ducha de un bienestar
acariciante

recomienzo el horario de la sonrisa
el calendario retrocede
                sobre mi viejo pensamiento

"El trabajo intelectual
perjudica la belleza del rostro" —Oscar Wilde

y como todo es relativo
                pongámosle un poco de belleza
a estos días heróicos
acribillados de números de acero   celuloides
        de cartas   etc   etc

yo tengo preso el sueño de la Vida
pájaro en jaula de hierro
                con una puertecita a la esperanza

el Sol sale todos los días
        de sus telarañas de nubes

15

morning's magnifying moon
duplicates the mathematical landscape
now everything receives a double percentage of Sun

my delicate body of a civilized woman
cloaked in neurasthenic haze
strips naked in the shower of
caressing well-being

the timetable of the smile begins again
the calendar races backward
                              over my former speculations

"Intellect destroys
the harmony of the face" —Oscar Wilde

since all is relative
        let's lend a bit of beauty
to these heroic days
riddled with steel numerals   celluloid
        letters   etc   etc

I hold prisoner the dream of Life
bird in an iron cage
        with a tiny door open to hope

every day the Sun breaks through
                              its cloud cobwebs

16

enormes tiras blancas de papel
la nieve trae mensajes del cielo
con la firma dorada de los rayos

el viento silba una tragicomedia
celestial

      que acompaña el bárbaro
jazz-band de los truenos

el escenario del cielo   de los cerros
de las casas enmudecidas de neblina
tiene los tonos clásicos de las grandes
tristezas:
      el gris en todas las variaciones
del mercado

los papeles blancos de la nieve
nos arrojan programas a la cara

más tarde
      el telón multicolor del
arcoíris   finaliza el espectáculo
y se abren los visillos de las nubes
para que el Sol salga a sonreír

16

voluminous flurries of paper
the snow brings news from the sky
signed by a gilt flourish of the rays

the wind sighs a celestial
tragicomedy

     accompanied by thunder's
barbarous jazz-band

the stage of the sky   of the hills
of the fog-silenced houses
has the classical tones of the great
sadnesses:
     the grey of all the stock market's
jitterings

white sheets of snow
hurl programs in our faces

later
     the multi-colored drop-curtain
of the rainbow   ends the spectacle
plush draperies of cloud draw back
to let in beaming Sun

AGUJA

detrás se han abierto
hondas zanjas de misterio

acaparas mis ideas
con hélices de neurastenia

todo tu clamor se perdió
vastamente en la tierra

representante de las Madres
recién son ciertos los puñales de María

tu último gesto
se ha colgado en la sombra borrosa
de la madrugada
delante de mis ojos
teje su telaraña de tristeza

¿hace cuántos días?
árboles
cohetes de estrellas
sobre las piedras refinadas del río
cataratas de sol
                sobre el primitivo y alegre paisaje

pero HOY solo estás tú
pequeña muerta dolorosa
raramente clavada en el fondo
del paisaje   como una cruz

NEEDLE

Behind me
deep trenches of mystery

whirling propellers
of apprehension blur my thoughts

such a clamor
disappearing in the world

archetypal Mother
only now Mary's daggers are real

your last gesture
hangs in dawn's
grey smudge
weaving before my eyes
its tissue of sadness

how many days since then?
trees
sky-rocketing stars
sunlight cascading
on polished riverstones
                on the primeval scenery of joy

TODAY you alone remain
tiny dolorous death
strangely pinned in the depth
of the landscape   like a cross

NADA
NADA DE TI
y sin embargo
en las antenas del cerebro
se han posado las golondrinas
tristes del
                recuerdo

yo las miro atenta
¿cuándo volarán?

el horizonte partido por el ayer
que no regresa
detrás de ti
                el Misterio echó sus redes

NOTHING
NO NEWS OF YOU
nevertheless
sad swallows of
                    m e m o r y
alight on the antenna of my mind

I watch them curiously
when will they fly off

the horizon shot through with
yesterdays that fail
to recede behind me
                    Mystery casts its nets

CARTÓN MORADO

CASUALIDAD
                    Madre de los desamparados
Es ya rojo todo el camino recorrido
Con tres jirones de alma menos
y esperando

Como si todavía hubiera providencia
Y, ¿aún no se me enturbia mi esmeralda ilimitada?
Me están llamando las lágrimas hace rato
se rebelan contra mi sequedad
Y lloro

Mañana habrá reventado un botón nuevo
con el calor de esta noche
Estoy sola
            Cómo te amo Soledad
grande vacío de la noche
cómo te he amado siempre
Generadora de mis mejores pensamientos
paño de lágrimas
confidente y refugio

PURPLE CARDBOARD

CHANCE
                    Mother of the dispossessed
All the traveled road is red now
With three scraps of soul less
and counting

As if divine providence existed
Is it possible my infinite emerald is still unclouded?
Not long ago tears called to me
rebelling against my aridity
And I wept

Tomorrow a fresh bud will appear
fostered by the heat of this night
I'm alone
                    How I love you Solitude
great blank of the night
how I have always loved you
Source of my best thoughts
cloth of tears
confidant and refuge

MÁSCARA

el rotundo perfil destacado
en la calavera amarfilada
de cuencas llenas por dos ojos de
vidrios   donde a veces
ponen sus iris unas lágrimas

Anticipo de muerte

Espejo inoportuno
de una víspera de festín macabro
Apretada en la camisa de fuerza
de la tierra
                        como la última
venganza de los hombres

Ah   ¡cuando el mar!
Con sus jardines de luz viva
sus peces tornasol
y su perenne canto
sostendría mi danza extasiada
por los siglos de los siglos

Amén

MASK

the sharply defined profile
of the ivory skull
with hollows for two glass eyes
where on occasion
tears pool in irises

Anticipation of death

Untimely mirror
on the eve of a macabre festivity
Bound by the straight-jacket
of the land
                    as if by the ultimate
revenge of men

Ah   someday the sea!
With its gardens of dazzling light
its iridescent fish
and perennial song
will sustain my ecstatic dance
throughout centuries of centuries

A m e n

17

quisiera perderme de mi misma
limbo de mi pensamiento
y haber perdido la mirada angustiosa
de mis ojos
para los pasos arrebatados por la muerte

Perderme de los hilos tensos
que el corazón tiende a los cuatro
puntos cardinales de la Vida

Saltar el círculo que me aprisiona
y en el que se debate
          serpiente cercada de llamas
mi juventud inútil

¡Perderse!   tendido vuelo
por sobre las agujas de las ciudades
más altas   por sobre el mar
como un globo cargado de oxígeno
que sueltan a merced de los vientos

L e j o s   Más allá de todas las distancias

          L e j o s   d e   m í

17

I want to lose myself from myself
limbo of my mind
I want to be rid of the anguished look in my eyes
as I await death's snatching step

To be free of the taut threads
the heart flings to the four
cardinal points of life

To leap from the imprisoning circle
where   snake ringed by fire
my idle youth combats itself

To lose myself!   extended in flight
above the spires of the cities
higher   above the sea
like a balloon swollen with oxygen
loosed to the mercy of winds

F a r   Beyond all distances

        F a r   f r o m   m y s e l f

18

orillas de la angustia
allí están todos los caminos salobres
como el mar

bajo la noche acobardada
letanía de remordimientos
tus manos arañan en las raíces del cerebro
y todas las zanjas interrogan
los ojos vacíos de la noche
su indiferencia paralítica

el mar hincha su lomo negro
como una montaña
            para mirar bien alto

y la emoción trepida sus motores
de angustia y de alegría
ante lo nuevo

2000 kilómetros fuera de la
R E A L I D A D

las antenas telepáticas
traen mensajes atrabiliarios

los contómetros señalan distancias
en los costados paralelos del presente
la muerte custodia

18

shores of anguish
there where every brackish road starts out
like the sea

unnerved by the cover of night
litany of regrets
your hands dig at the roots of my brain
every furrow interrogates
night's vacant eyes
its paralytic indifference

the sea juts its black spine
like a mountain
        to look from on high

emotion races its motors
of anguish and exhilaration
before the new

2000 kilometers apart from
R E A L I T Y

telepathic antennas
bring bilious messages

comptometers signal distances
on parallel sides of the present
death watches

ESPUMAS

hoy me sube una maldición a los labios
desde el frio de mi corazón
Se crispan todas las uñas
para incrustarse en mi orgullo

Porque todo ha sido vano
y mis palabras inútiles
y se ha dormido el fantasma de mi voluntad
para dejar crecer a la otra Sombra
que hoy se proyecta
              s o b r e   t o d a
                  MI VIDA

Fragilidad de mis manos incapaces
para crujir sobre la angustia de mi corazón
y dejar que me suba a los labios
            ajenjo de impotencia
la palabra sin anestesias

SEA FOAM

a curse flickers on my lips today
arisen from my icy heart
Every fingernail poised
to dig into my pride

Because it's all come to nothing
nothing I said made a difference
the phantom of my volition fell asleep
leaving the other to grow   the S h a d o w
to fall
      on e v e r y t h i n g
        my L I F E

Fragility of my useless hands
they crack over my heartache
unable to keep from my lips
      bitter herb of helplessness
this speech without anesthesia

VIERNES 13

d o l o r
¿luego esta noche ha sido larga?
¿Cuándo te clavaré
las garras de mis uñas
en tus carnes de cuervo negro?

Ardida está mi frente
y mis manos   heladas

Una noche de insomnio
y la vejez de mis veinte años
acentuada

TU   mala raíz   amarga
te voy a descentrar de mis entrañas
que ya hace tiempo sopla la Tragedia
por mis campos

Estoy amarga   amarga
tengo en el paladar   raíz   tu savia

Y hay un hondo dolor
seco   sin lágrimas

Un dolor
que casi es ebriedad

FRIDAY THE 13TH

p a i n
will this night not end?
When will I claw
with my sharp nails
your black crow flesh?

Burning forehead
my hands   are ice

Insomniac night
and the old age of my twenty years
intensifies

YOU   bad root   bitter
I will dislodge you from my entrails
for some time now Tragedy
has swept through my fields

I'm bitter   bitter
on my palate   root   is your sap

There's a deep pain
dry   tearless

Pain
that is almost inebriation

EL MANDATO

habrá necesidad de domar a las fieras
y sujetar al muro de la Vida
las más fuertes cadenas

Y no soñar

Durante un lapso grande
ser un cerebro y una VOLUNTAD

Abrir los ojos como dos receptores
y aprisionar la Vida
redondamente en la mirada
Y ser por los que nunca han sido
como el Sol por todas las noches
como el Agua por las sequedades

Así ha de ser este HOY
Porque el HOY es la Vida
Porque el Mañana está detrás
de las fronteras de la Vida

Así HOY
Este H O Y majestuoso y terrible
al que se debe todo:
            hasta la muerte

Este Hoy
            que está gritándonos:
                  CUMPLID!

THE COMMAND

our animal spirits must be broken
fastened to the wall of life
by iron chains

All reverie suppressed

For a good long time
be a brain and a WILL

Opening our eyes like two receivers
to capture Life
entirely in our gaze
To be for those who have never fully lived
like Sun at night
like Water during drought

That is how this TODAY must be
For TODAY is Life
Tomorrow is beyond
the frontiers of Life

TODAY
This majestic and terrible   T O D A Y
to which everything
        even death is owed

This Today
        screaming at us:
                DUTY COMMANDS YOU

como si todo hubiera sido estéril
y quisiera vernos rehabilitar
las horas vacuas
que como ramas tristes se arrancaron de
su árbol
                    y le faltan

as if all our efforts had so far not been serious
and Time wanted back
those wasted hours
which like sad branches were torn from
its tree

         and which it misses

MAR DE ALEGRÍA

Yo soy un mar porque no hubiera sido un río
Un mar sin cauces
de verdes alegrías
y de profundas soledades
Un mar abarcador
de la Vida y la Muerte
del que parten y al que confluyen
todas las fuerzas de la Vida

Yo soy un mar como ese mar en calma
que ven mis ojos
y que ciñe la Tierra
con su soberbio beso blando

Yo soy un Mar
pupilas de crepúsculo
y voz de aurora
Como ese mar azul
al que yo desperté en mi primer viaje
Aquel mar de los brazos abiertos
de la perenne juventud
donde se posa mi Esperanza
gaviota blanca
con las pupilas rosas
Yo soy un Mar

Génesis de la Vida

JOYOUS SEA

I'm a sea since I could never have been a river
An unchanneled sea
of green merriments
and solitary depths
A sea embracing
Life and Death
out of which all vital force
emerges and to which it returns

I am a sea like that becalmed ocean
I see before me
skirting the Land
with its gentle sovereign kiss

I am a Sea
eyes of dusk
voice of early light
Like that indigo ocean
I woke to on my first voyage
That sea with the open arms
of perennial youth
Where my Hope alights
white seagull
with dawn-colored eyes
I am a Sea

Genesis of Life

LA TRAGEDIA COMÚN

un solo pensamiento
como una barra taladrando el cráneo

Un solo pensamiento

El dolor en las sienes
en los ojos
en las neuronas

UNO SOLO

Tan largos días

Qué agudo es el dolor
de un pensamiento solo

Como si estuviera colgada de una mano
pendiendo en un abismo
así es esta locura
fatigante
de un solo pensamiento

Arañando quisiera desentrañármelo
hendiendo en la gris masa de mi cráneo
las uñas afiladas

Porque estoy obsedida
hasta la máxima expresión del grito

COMMON TRAGEDY

A single thought
like a spear thrust deep into my brain

A s i n g l e t h o u g h t

My temples throb
and my eyes
          my neurons

                O N L Y O N E

Such drawn-out days

How excruciating
the one thought

As if suspended
by a hand above a chasm
you can see how this madness
                of a single thought
is exhausting

If only my sharpened nails
could extract it
from the grey matter of my skull

Because I am obsessed
to the maximum intensity   I cry out

Ah
      y que se desvanezca
      junto con la voz

A la media noche
parece que es su mano la que me despierta
Dolorosamente lo cobijo en mis ojos
y así largas horas

Con la mañana   junto con mis párpados
se levanta en el fondo de mi cráneo
Y a veces hasta sueño con él

Que cansancio

Yo siempre tuve ideas   mares
móviles como olas
fugaces, volanderas
de ágiles alas

      Pero esta piedra dura
de un solo pensamiento
me está aplastando el cráneo
          M i r a d m e
              Tengo en los ojos la tragedia

Oh
        let that cry fade
        and this voice

At midnight
I think it is his hand that awakens me
Painfully my eyes hold it
for hours this goes on

In the morning   eyelids stir
from deep in my brain it arises
Sometimes I even dream of it

It's enervating

I always had ideas   seas
mobile as waves
elusive, lifting
on agile wings

        But this hard stone
of a single thought
is ruining my mind
                Look at me
                    Tragedy is in my eyes

CANTO 1

crepúsculo
sonrisa de colores
para acompañar mi alegría

Qué bellamente decoras
mi panorama espiritual
espigado de oro
en esta maravillosa fiesta de
mi Alegría

Gran pandereta
Juventud   Alegría
el arco iris de tus flecos
agita su orquesta sobre mi
corazón

Por los arcos de mis ojos
pasan los ejércitos triunfales de la
VIDA

Y mis cabellos rojos
banderas de alegría
se agitan bajo el SOL

SONG 1

sunset
beaming colors
to accompany my happiness

How beautifully you decorate
my spiritual panorama
gold-spangled
in this marvelous fiesta of
Lightheartedness

Great tambourine
Youth   Gaiety
the rainbow of your fringes
agitates its orchestra upon my
heart

Through the arches of my eyes
LIFE'S
triumphal armies march

And my red hair
banner of happiness
waves under the SUN

EL MAR DISTANTE

los barcos van al norte van al sur
tristeza de tus ojos que van hacia
el mismo centro de mi espíritu

Los barcos hijos de la Angustia
ellos mismos la Angustia
con su cargamento de esperanzas
inútiles   anclan en los puertos
mendigos portadores de oro
recojen dolor y dejan dolor

Oh   miradas de los viajeros donde el
mar puso la trágica ansiedad de sus
sirenas míticas
De los viajeros que no logran llegar

Miradas que desfilan por los muelles
vacíos donde no está quien las espera
Miradas como las algas   frías
Lívidos farolillos de colores que
pasean su procesión fantástica sobre
la fantasía del Mar

DISTANT SEA

ships steam north steam south
sadness of your eyes as they approach
my spirit's core

Ships children of Anguish
Anguish itself   with their cargo
of futile hopes
they drop anchor in ports
beggars hauling gold
they load and unload sorrows

Oh   the searching eyes of travelers
where the sea pools the tragic disquiet
of its mythical sirens
Travelers who never arrive

Gazes shifting over vacant wharves
where no one is waiting
Gazes like seaweed   cold
Faintly glowing colored lanterns
gliding in fantastic procession
over the Sea's fantasia

POEMAS CLAROSCUROS

Un pálido reflejo
un reflejo amarillo
empalideció más aún mi semblante
y tuve así un color llama de cirio
a la luz clara
                    un color de muerto

entre las cuencas oscuras
brillábanme los ojos nocharniegos
Enmarcaba la frente en la parda bruma
los enmarañados cabellos

Esta noche   la otra   la otra
Todas las noches hubieron meditaciones
                    y l á g r i m a s
Esta noche más junto a mi alma
he clavado las hondas interiores pupilas
en el hueco por donde se cae al Vacío
          a rodar
                    a rodar
sin pararse jamás
Después de pasar por la vida
llevando prendidas
Todas las garras en la carne
          todas las fieras en el alma
Afueteados de duda

Más junto de mi alma esta noche
he querido   g r i t a r

CHIAROSCURO

Pale reflection
a sallow reflection
my face in the mirror more pale
wan color of a candle
burning in daylight
                    waxen color of death

from shadowy hollows
my night-wandering eyes gleam
The dark fog of my tangled hair
frames my brow

Tonight   over and over
Each night are meditations
              and   t e a r s
This night nearer my soul
I've fixed my inmost eyes on a void
through which Emptiness drops
              to reel
                        to reel
never coming to rest
Having passed through life
bearing claw-marks
body and soul have been mauled
Flayed by doubt

My spirit raw tonight
I want to   s c r e a m

EL VIENTO DE SU SOMBRA

tu presencia me martilló en las sienes
y en el corazón
             hasta el recuerdo vivo

Qué jadeo el de esta Noche
en la pantalla rosa
donde quema sus alas mi alegría
Esta noche materializada
             que detiene a la aurora

¿Quien eres tú?   Ya no recuerdo
Ni tus facciones, ni tus ojos

T a n   s o l o   t u   m i r a d a
a través de todo
             limpia como un cristal oscuro
brillándome

Tu mirada buena, dulce y triste
tu hermana-mirada
que siempre tiene un " v e n "

Ah emoción de esta noche
hermana de la noche pasada
Recuerdo vivo y palpitante
cual si estuvieran tus dos manos en mi frente

Angustia de todos los días
¿Qué me traes?   alma triste

HIS SHADOW'S WIND

your presence batters my temples
beats in my heart
          throughout my living memory

Breathless Night
on its roseate screen
the wings of my joy burn up
This incarnate night
          holds back the dawn

Who were you?   I can't remember
your features   not even your eyes

O n l y   y o u r   g a z e
remains through it all
          clean like dark glass
shining for me

Your kind gaze   gentle and sad
your sister-gaze
always with that expression "come to me"

Ah such emotion tonight
sister of the night before
A visceral memory
as if your hands held my face

Anguish of these days
What is it you bring me?   Sadness

anunciadora de dolor
   ¿Qué me traes?
     Mírame cómo tiemblo
HERMANA H e r m a n a hermana
¿Porqué he de temerle a tu presencia que amo?

herald of pain
      What is it you bring?
         See how I'm trembling
SISTER   s i s t e r   sister
Why must I fear the presence that I love?

El Desfile de las Miradas

a Serafín Delmar

Parade of Glances

for Serafín Delmar

EL VIAJERO DE TODOS LOS MARES

yo era triste
como los pájaros de media Noche
acostados en las tinieblas

    Como las punas sin árboles
de frente a los vientos fríos de
la Costa

    triste como los fuertes
y como los vencidos   cuando
empieza la muerte anticipada de la
    I n d i f e r e n c i a

A M O R   yo estaba triste
se ensangrentaron mis costados
    se murieron mis peces de colores
y la perfidia número UNO bamboleó
mi equilibrio
    a la atracción del abismo

Y los pájaros de media noche
rondaron el naufragio de mi
Corazón   en las arenas abandonadas

PERO LLEGASTE
    TÚ   para quien mis brazos
se abrieron en cruz
y las arañas del sueño tejieron
la seda infinita de la amnesia

SAILOR OF EVERY SEA

I was sad
like nocturnal birds
nested in mist

      Like treeless plains
scoured by icy winds of the
Coast

      sad like the strong
and like the vanquished   at the first sign
of the anticipated death that is
      I n d i f f e r e n c e

L O V E   I felt sad
my sides bled
      my fish of colors died
dishonesty   above ALL else
unbalanced me
      drew me to an abyss

Midnight birds
circled my Heart's shipwreck
        on desolate sands

BUT YOU CAME
      YOU   my arms opened
in a cross for you
dream-spiders wove
amnesia's infinite silks

TÚ   conquistador ilusionado
de mis tribus salvajes de tristeza
donde llevaste la religión de una
alegría   nueva como los aeroplanos
sobre las selvas vírgenes

Hoy el traje de nuestros almas
es el arcoíris de la sonrisa

YOU   eager conqueror
of my sadness   its savage tribes
you introduced the religion of
a joy   new like airplanes
skimming virgin forests

Today the dress of our souls
is a beaming rainbow

NOCHE

qué grandes suenan las voces de los perros
ladrando a los ecos

Pero mi cerebro tiene todos los ruidos
que se han perdido en la Noche

Estoy lejos de la realidad
como en un baño de espacios

Yo llegué al último círculo
y sobre mi corazón flotaba
                TU   NOMBRE

La mañana está lejos
c o m o   T Ú
con puentes de oscuridad

eternidad de la Noche
                y de tu ausencia

Mis lágrimas iluminan mi cara en sombras
donde se ha zincograbado
tu última mirada

Pero oye
            todos los ruidos se vacían
de mi cerebro y se reparten en los
rincones profundos de la Noche

NIGHT

explosive yapping of dogs
barking at echoes

My brain retains every sound
that's lost in the night

Far from reality
as in a bath of space

I've attained the last circle
floating on my heart is
            Y O U R   N A M E

Morning is far away
l i k e   YOU
beyond spans of darkness

eternity of Night
            and your absence

Lustrous tears illumine my shadowed face
where your last glance
is metallically engraved

Listen
        all the noises stream
from my brain and seek their place
in deep recesses of the Night

y sólo quedan sobre el telón oscuro
de mi conciencia las luces de bengala
que dibujan el reclamo de
        t u   n o m b r e

nothing remains on the black curtain
of my consciousness but flashing lights
rippling in the electrical attraction of
     y o u r   n a m e

LAS MIRADAS AUSENTES

mírame
Mi neurastenia de miradas
como de mar
como de largos viajes

Ve la tortura mendiga de mis ojos
cazando al vuelo la mariposa viajera
de tu mirada

      N a d a   m á s

Las miradas me obseden
Querría todas las pupilas
las verdes, las doradas, las negras
para tapizar las paredes de mi vida

Y les tengo miedo
Por eso me odian   Lorraine   los ojos
Mis ojos dorados de serpiente
en el estuche abierto de mis verdes ojeras

Mis ojos que atraerían todas las miradas
como llamas de colores alrededor
de mi Vida

Líbrame de este mal

Ah la tortura acariciante de tu mirada
Tus rayos X que te muestran

ABSENT GLANCES

look at me
Neurasthenia of gazes
restless as sea-water
and long voyages

See the pleading torment of my eyes
as they trace the flitting butterfly
of your gaze

      O n l y   t h a t

Glances obsess me
I'm enamored of every eye color
green   gold   black
decorating the walls of my life

And I fear them
That's why they hate me   Lorelei eyes
My reptilian topaz eyes
set in my dark circles' open jewel case

My eyes would attract every gaze
like iridescent flames
flickering about my Life

Deliver me from this evil

Oh the caressing torture of your gaze
Your X-rays that reveal

mi corazón desnudo

MÍRAME!

estoy en el umbral de tus ojos

my naked heart

SEE ME

I'm here on the threshold of your eyes

SALMO DE AMOR

TE AMO
como una salmodia triste
encendidos todos sus soles
como una augusta blasfemia
estriada de sangre

Desde mis subterráneos
sale esa sola voz
       C I E G A
       como un Lázaro
envuelta en vahos cálidos
rasgada su mortaja de silencio

Pero mas tarde habrá perdido toda su sonoridad
en el ruido de las grandes ciudades
en la angustia de los puertos atravesados
de promesas
           y en el afán multicolor de
los barcos dejados a prisa

Mas su eco-hebra de seda suave
atará el corazón al pensamiento
para establecer la corriente del
       Recuerdo

      EL ÚNICO
que tenderá su red
          sobre todas mis vidas muertas

LOVE CANTICLE

I LOVE YOU
like a sad canticle
a burnt offering of suns
a solemn sacrilege
sprinkled with blood

Out of the depths
a sole voice
       BLIND
       like a Lazarus
wrapped in warm vapors
a shroud of silence is ripped off

A sonority soon to be lost
in the roar of great cities
in the anguish of ports
traversed with promises
           in the multicolored exhilaration
of steamships heading out

Yet its silken echo-thread
will tether the heart to thought
the current of   M e m o r y
will start to flow

    THE ONLY THING
that can cast its net
         to haul in my dead lives

Pero HOY
	temblorosa y alegremente
oye la voz de mis entrañas:

       TE   AMO

But TODAY
      trembling   happily
I hear the voice of my body

      I LOVE YOU

POEMAS DE LA NOCHE

todos los ruidos se incrustaban en la gran boca de la
Noche   que destilaba su tinta sobre la conciencia
universal para trocar en belleza los pecados que el Día
desnuda de sus máscaras y deja ver con todas sus lepras

    Oh Noche maga   encendido carbón de deseo
para tu palpitante mármol negro son mis oscuros
lirios y mis rojas azucenas

Así le salía un canto a la Noche porque el Mar de
sus deseos desbordándose sobre su ser   le calcinaba
    y la madre Soledad   tan amada   le había puesto
alrededor del cuello   cadenas irrompibles   sus dos
tremendos brazos

    Hermana Noche   Madre Noche bien haya tu
amplio camino de sombra para los reflectores de mis ojos

    Todo en ti se prestigia y se aureola de una sombra
divina   Y el amor   el Magnífico Interrogante erguido
en púrpura al Misterio   encuentra su amplia respuesta

Noche fecunda madre de Belleza:

    TÓMAME

porque la Noche perfumaba su corazón   maravillaba la
suave caricia de sus manos y encendía los vidrios oscuros
de sus ojos en dos claras luciérnagas

POEMS OF THE NIGHT

every sound inlaid in the great mouth of Night
its ink streaming over universal consciousness
making beautiful the sins Day unmasks laying bare
every sore

    Oh enchantress Night   glowing coal of desire
my dark irises and scarlet lilies are destined for
your pulsing black marble   So the Night

poured forth a song   for the Sea of unbridled desires
became a flood   charred the Night   Mother
Solitude   dearly beloved   draped unbreakable
chains about your neck   two tremendous arms

    Sister Night   Mother Night   lay wide your path
of shadow for my reflector eyes

    In you all is privileged in an aura of sacred shade
And love   Magnificent Interrogator   borne aloft in
purple to Mystery   there finds its full response

    Night fertile mother of Beauty:

    T A K E   M E

the heart of Night drenched in fragrance enthralling
caress of her hands   the illumined black windows of
her eyes   two blinking fireflies

TOMA MI CORAZÓN

Pero esta Noche   A m a n t e   los cálidos anillos de
tus brazos no adornan el incensario vivo de mi cuerpo

Y ESTOY TRISTE

TAKE MY HEART

But Tonight   L o v e r   the warm rings of your
arms do not adorn the swaying censer of my body

AND I AM SAD

AUSENCIA

embriaguez de dolor y de amor
tan cercana a la muerte
hoy agonizan mis llamadas
frente al espectro de tu sonrisa
que ya es apenas
                    un instante muerto
ante tu realidad presente
desconocida para mí

Yo ignoro   t o d o
hasta los aletazos de la Tragedia
trazando sus círculos sobre mi cabeza

Solo sé en esta hora
                    de proyecciones infinitas
q u e   AMO   y   e s t o y

                    S O L A

y que ha muerto la Tierra

ABSENCE

misery and love intoxicate me
so like annihilation
my cries agonize
seeing the phantom of your smile
barely
                    a dead instant
in the face of your current reality
unknown to me today

I'm ignorant of   e v e r y t h i n g
even of Tragedy's wing-beats
circling above my head

All I know in this hour
                of infinite projections
i s   t h a t   I   LOVE

            a n d   a m   A L O N E

and the Earth has died

PUENTES

SI   VIDA
Mi blasfemia cortada
y dispersa en el dolor de mis células
cerebrales   como vidrios rotos
tiranizados
por una alegre puñalada de luz
riéndose en su arco iris de colores

H o y   e s   l a   n o c h e
que desnuda mis nervios

Y la montaña de mi deseo
se hunde sobre mi corazón
e s t r e p i t o s a m e n t e
hasta dejarme
                    sin deseo

Arriba la señal roja de la amenaza
por venir

                    Mañana   Hoy

        pero hoy no vivo
la Vida me da las espaldas
y del Ayer salta al Mañana

Hoy es tan sólo una laguna fría
que no calienta ni sus besos
y en donde tristemente naufraga

BRIDGES

YES   LIFE
Blasphemy slashed
and dispersed in the pain of
cerebral cells   like shattered panes
tyrannized
by a merry fistful of light
its shimmering laugh of colors

T o d a y   is   t h e   n i g h t
that strips my nerves

Mountainous desire
a rock slide in my heart
a   d e a f e n i n g   c r a s h
and I am left
                        desireless

Up goes the red signal of future
danger

                    Tomorrow   Today

            but today I'm not alive
Life ignores me
Yesterday leaps straight into Tomorrow

Today is an icy pool
that even his kisses cannot warm
where the blond and emerald butterfly

sobre rojos gladiolos campesinos
la rubia y verde mariposa de mi
e s p e r a n z a

AYER   MAÑANA

A veces
parece que la Vida me resucita
por las noches
mientras alumbran los cristales verdeamarillo
de sus ojos sin   v o z

Ah
si supieran hablar
su extraña música hermanada a mi corazón
Sin la traición amarga de
mi carne — mármol

Pero NO

        of my   h o p e   is dashed
sadly colliding with the crimson
gladioli of country fields

            YESTERDAY   TOMORROW

Sometimes
it seems that Life revives me
at night
when the yellow-green crystals of its
v o i c e l e s s   eyes grow bright

Ah
if only they could sing
their strange music   twin sister to my heart
Without the bitter treason of
my flesh — marble

            But NO

ÚLTIMA INVOCACIÓN A LA LUNA

mariposa de luz   Noctámbula incolora
besa la roja raíz de este amor-sol
                 lleno de s o m b r a
lleno de tenebrosos rincones
que camina tambaleándose
por las encrucijadas de la locura

Envuélveme en tu palidez
desde los iris de mis ojos
que el amor fosforece como gemas extrañas
ponles tu opalescencia de astro muerto
hasta mis manos amarfiladas
lirios de decadencia
perfume tembloroso de su boca

Porque nunca te he amado
dame un motivo de gratitud:
         O P Á C A M E

Vidrios de mi emoción
por donde tantos ojos aguaitan mi éxtasis
frente al gran cuadro robado:

L A   V I D A

         Y   E L   A M O R

FINAL INVOCATION TO THE MOON

sunlight's butterfly is nocturnal now
colorless   it sips at the blood-root of this
daylight love   brimming with
d a r k n e s s   shadowy corners
at the crossroads of madness
reeling

Bathe me in your ashen rays
from my irises   phosphoresced
by love into strange jewels
to my ivory hands   decadent lilies
Pour down your dead planet's
opalescence
tremulous fragrance of your mouth

Because I've never loved you
give me a motive for gratitude
       H I D E   M E

Windows of my passion
so many eyes await my rapture
I stand before
the great plundered canvas

of   L I F E
              and   L O V E

CRISPACIONES

NO DOLOR
Yo morderé tu cabeza
y tus anillos dejaran de apretarme

Derrepente   pirata de ojos claros
le vi delante de la sorpresa
de mis ojos

Hoy se roba mis lágrimas
diamantadas de alegría

Por eso me castigas con tus fríos anillos
Dolor   espiral ardorosa
Pero sus manos
que se llevan mis lágrimas
son las dulces verónicas
para mi corazón lleno de espinas
viajero de la ruta de Cristo

Desajústate un poco
serpiente de mis noches
y de mis días

        Quiero ser feliz
sin el espasmo de tus anillos
bebiéndome la sidra de sus ojos

Ya habrá tiempo Dolor
de que te ajustes tanto a mí

TENSION

PAIN NO
I'll bite your head off
your constricting rings will release me

Out of the blue he appeared
clear-eyed pirate
surprising my eyes

Today he steals my tears
diamond-dusted in delight

That's why you punish me with your icy rings
Fiery coils of   Pain
Yet his hands dry my tears
like Veronica's veils
soothing my thorn-pierced heart
traveler of Christ's stations

Anaconda of my nights and days
Release me   if only a little

                  I want to be happy   free
from the spasm of his coils
while the cider of his eyes
drains away

There will be time Pain
so perfectly will you adjust to me

que seamos uno   los dos
y para siempre
con mis ojos
empapados de éter

we will be one   the two of us
forever
and my eyes
will be drenched in ether

TRAMOS DE LUZ

y bien   la Noche
Sobre el pálido Corazón
aguza todos sus cuervos mi pensamiento

Cuántos escombros
                    para llorar sin lágrimas

SI   Pero alrededor
        murallas encendidas
            c u s t o d i a n   t u s   b e s o s

Primero son los largos pinos de sus sombras
sin ojos

                emergiendo la tuya como todas
PERO CON TU ÚLTIMA MIRADA

Luego   cremadores de ultraconciencia
las murallas iluminadas
perfilan nuestras dos sombras erguidas
en la crucifixión inacabable de nuestras miradas
            temblorosas por el espasmo
de su martirio sobre el madero del AMOR

            NUESTRAS DOS SOMBRAS
            ETERNIZANDO EL
            HOY

SEGMENTS OF LIGHT

well then   Night
On my pallid Heart
not a crow that isn't pecking at my thoughts

What a lot of trash
          to mourn dry-eyed

YES   But all around me
     burning ramparts
         g u a r d   y o u r   k i s s e s

First the towering pines of our eyeless
shadows

         yours emerging among others
BUT WITH YOUR RECENT GAZE

Then   crematoria of ultra-consciousness
on illumined walls
our shadows loom in profile
in the endless crucifixion of our glances
     trembling in the spasm
of martyrdom on the wood of LOVE

     OUR TWO SHADOWS
      ETERNALIZING
       TODAY

enmascarado de ironía

MÁSCARAS   m á s c a r a s   máscaras
Nosotros que llevamos el Espíritu
como un fruto en las manos abiertas

¿Qué trozo de la conciencia tenemos
aun esclava?

    Hoy se duele mi corazón
porque todavía no halla su eco
en el credo sagrado de la

       L I B E R T A D

masked with irony

MASKS   m a s k s   masks
We who bear the Spirit
like a fruit in our open hands

What trace of consciousness is left to us
still enslaved?

           Today my heart grieves
having not yet found its echo
in the sacred creed of

           LIBERTY

CAMINO ALUCINANTE

ahora perfumadme
claveles
porque me siento triste
apesar de mi fiebre

Daos a mis arañas de marfil
y a mi coral de histeria
Daos a mis pupilas de reptil
estriadas de fosforescencias

Claveles
en dónde habrán adormideras?
Quiero para mis ojos
para mi olfato
y para mis arañas de marfil

Oh Tarde muerta
¿hacia dónde me llevas?
al camino de mis verdes ojeras
y de mis corneas violadas

MESMERIZING PATH

perfume me
carnations
because I feel sad
despite being feverish

Yield to my ivory spiders
to my frantic corals
Yield to these reptilian eyes
phosphorescence-flecked

Carnations
but where will I find poppies
I want them for my eyes
my nostrils
and for my ivory spiders

O listless dusk
where are you leading me
Along the path of
my greenish dark-circles
Along the way of
my violated corneas

CANTO 5

como otra vez tu sonrisa se hermana
a la de los panoramas idos
allá   sobre las frágiles agujas
de nuestro amor aventurero
        brújula cerebral

en los cuatro lados totales: a b u r r i m i e n t o
con el pálido Sol abrigado entre sábanas
y los vidrios de colores empañados   iguales
abajo la alharaca del río
y el campo miserable
para los ojos desorbitados de deseo

la soledad en medio de tanta gente
siempre somos extranjeros en la tierra

la inútil campana del corazón
que anuncia el arribo de alguien
que siempre resulta   n a d i e

      celuloide ahumado
frutos del trópico
      alegría de los pájaros
la luna ha barrido todas las estrellas
hundida en su baño de leche

la luna   decadencia anacrónica
del panorama sideral
como los poetas clásicos y los románticos
en el panorama de los nuevos artistas

SONG 5

once again your smile
matches that of vanished landscapes
there   under the delicate needles
of our errant love's
          cerebral compass

in all four directions: b o r e d o m
with a whitish Sun screened by bed-sheets
and tarnished windowpanes   it's all the same
under the racket of the river
and the stony field
to eyes disoriented by desire

alone in the midst of crowds
always we are strangers on the earth

the heart's cracked bell
tolls the approach of someone
yet no one ever   a r r i v e s

          smoky film
tropical fruits
          exhilarated birds
the moon has swept away the stars
afloat in her milky bath

the moon   anachronistic decadence
of the celestial panorama
like the classic and romantic poets
in the landscape of modern artists

sumergida en un baño de spleen
quisiera cerrar los ojos y estar
a   la   vuelta   del
        mundo

submerged in a bath of spleen
I want to close my eyes and be
o n   t h e   o t h e r   s i d e
of   the   world

ARCOS

hoy creo todo falso
en este amor de humo
desde los dos estanques
vidriados de tus ojos
               donde se inmovilizan mis pupilas
hasta la realidad emocionada
de tus dos manos infinitas

solo es verdad la angustia de esta noche
palpable entre mis manos frías
y el llanto que me cae para adentro
y este deseo de pedir   p e r d ó n

Ambiguas esmeraldas de mi risa
Decoración fastuosa de mis cenefas de tristeza
como dos ojos verdes que han visto mucho el mar
y que sienten nostalgias de dormir en su seno

          Bendita seas Hora
      porque afirmas la angustia
de que este amor solo es un sueño

ARCS

Today everything
in this smoky love
seems false to me
from the two glazed pools of your eyes
                    where my pupils are immobilized
to the thrilled reality
of your infinite hands

anguish is the only true thing tonight
palpable in cold hands
in the sob that falls through me
in this desire to ask   f o r g i v e n e s s

Ambiguous emeralds of my laughter
Lavish decoration of this foam-laced sadness
like two green eyes that have looked and looked
at the sea and that feel nostalgic
yearning to sleep in its arms

         Bless you Hour
      because you affirm my suffering
I know this love is unreal

LAS COLINAS MORADAS

mis ojos destilan amor
y mis labios plegados aprisionan tus últimos
besos que se van
se van con tus labios   con tus ojos sin noche
con tus manos portadoras de agonía

       Yo   no   quiero   estar
          triste

Tómame de la mano para jugar con la alegría
Y echemos al viento las flores violentas de
nuestra juventud

N O C H E   para qué son tus brazos de terciopelo?

Tus ojos son los "espejos alucinados" que mantienen
en éxtasis mi vida

Desde las aguas quietas del espejo me miran
mis ojos tristes

Y el triángulo que divide mis cejas reta al
Destino y la Noche   fosos sin puente
      entre TU y YO

Y me duermo pensando que me tienen tus brazos

PURPLE HILLS

my eyes distill love
and my pursed lips imprison your last
kisses that slip away
disappear with your lips   your nightless eyes
with your hands bearers of agony

       I   do   not   want   to
            be   sad

Take my hand let's sport with joy
Let's toss to the wind the violent blossoms
of our youth

N I G H T   what use are your velvet arms?

Your eyes are the "hallucinated mirrors"
that suspend my life in ecstasy

From the mirror's quiet waters my sad eyes
look back

The triangle between my eyebrows challenges
Destiny and Night   chasms with no bridge
        between   YOU   and   ME

I fall asleep thinking I am in your arms

FILM VERMOUTH

tristes lagunas
para bañarse los luceros fríos
Yo estaba enferma de mi propia
incertidumbre

La duda ablanda a martillazos lentos
Y tu duda de mí
me hace dudar de mí

Con mis ojos atravesados de aceritos de miedo
en el crepúsculo final de mis ojeras
— media hora para la procesión de la Noche —
temblando de mi misma
y pidiendo socorro contra mí

Y TÚ eres todo
ilusionista en mi teatro de guiñol
La cuerda tesante de la última prueba
se pasaría con serenidad
si tus ojos terribles no anunciarán que voy
a caer

Ah equilibrista de la Vida
Yo quisiera gritarme
         "cáete de una vez"
y pavonar de sangre las baldosas
bajo tus ojos centinelas

FILM VERMOUTH: COCKTAIL HOUR SHOW

sad lagoons
bathing icy stars
I am sick
of my own uncertainty

Doubt's slow hammering
unnerves me
your doubt of me
makes me doubt myself

With my eyes pierced by tiny blades of fear
in the final dusk of their dark-circles
—half hour for the Evening promenade—
trembling unsteadily
pleading for help against myself

AND YOU are everything
master of my puppet theater
Tight-rope of the ultimate test
I'd walk it calmly
if your terrible eyes
did not announce my fall

Ah high-wire acrobat of Life
I want to scream
          "fall, get it over with"
spatter the paving stones with blood
under your sentinel eyes

bajo tus manos que poseen la central
de mis nervios

ilusionista de mi angustia

YO TE BESO LAS MANOS

under your hands that own the
powerhouse of my nerves

magician of my anguish

I KISS YOUR HANDS

ANGUSTIA

un día se ahogó para siempre
La roja luz dio un vuelco
Ahora todavía está caliente el sitio
                pero ya no hay fuego

Un día crujieron todas mis vigas

Estabas en todas partes   cerca
Yo con los ojos atentos
con las manos atentas y la boca

Ahora ya estás en otra parte   L e j o s

Y los ojos míos semicerrados en ensueño
Y la boca triste
              y las manos caídas
Y no se qué presiento

Un día se ahogó para siempre
Yo alcé los brazos rígidos y te pedí aire
Aire   Tal vez hubiera tiempo

Tú no oías

           Y se ahogó para siempre

ANGUISH

one day it died forever
A burning light switched off
It's still hot here
                but there's no fire

One day all my beams cracked

Your presence used to envelop me
lingering   intimately near
my eyes alert   and my hands and mouth

It's gone now   You are far away

Eyelids closing in daydream
mouth downcast
                    hands folded in my lap
A vague presentiment

It's over
I raised insistent arms and asked you for air
Air   There may still be time

You didn't hear

                    And it was over forever

GRITO

HERMANOS   aquí estamos
palabra ésta bañada en mi sangre
yo la amo sobre la palabra

c o m p a ñ e r o

mi soledad arañó en todos los rincones
para encontrar esta palabra
crucificada y altiva

¿cuántos pueden decirla?

rojo escalón de la vida
vaciemos todo nuestro caudal humano
para regar la conciencia de piedra
lámpara iluminada de amor
cómo escupen negras lágrimas
a la cara del cielo
todas las bocas de la acción
donde no saben llorar los esclavos
          telarañas de miedo
                    vitriolo de las almas
la cobardía sigue tatuando las espaldas

          PROCESIÓN DE HOMBRES TRISTES

aquí estamos nosotros
y nuestras grandes banderas
          de alegría libertaria

CRY

BROTHERS   here we are
this word bathed in blood
this word I cherish above the word

c o m p a ñ e r o

my loneliness in every corner
to find this noble martyred word

how many can say it?

red stairwell of experience
let's drain every human reservoir
to irrigate a stony consciousness
lamp burning with love

mouths of action
how they spit black tears at the sky

the enslaved don't know how to weep
snares of fear
                souls scathed by vitriol
timidity still leaves its stamp on backs

    MARCH OF SAD MEN

here we are
with our great banners
      of freedom-loving happiness

Note on the Spanish text

When Magda Portal prepared a selected poems, *Constancia del Ser* (Constancy of Being, 1965), she modified the layout of many of the poems, including thirty-one poems from *Una esperanza y el Mar*. The formatting changes she made represented Magda's later preference, so I've taken the liberty of using those versions and applying this formating style to the poems from the 1927 collection that did not appear in *Constancia del Ser*. Mostly she suppressed punctuation, spare to begin with, and substituted spaces for her liberal use of dashes in the 1927 volume. The usage of "i" in place of "y" was also abandoned. The final stanza of poem "18" is suppressed in the 1965 collection; here the original version appears.

Translator's Acknowledgments

Translation and presentation of the Spanish text of *Una esperanza y el Mar* are by the kind permission of the late Magda Portal and of Rocío Adriana Revolledo Pareja, The Estate of Magda Portal.

I am grateful to Rocío Revolledo for her friendship and indispensibly thoughtful assistance with all aspects of my work on Magda Portal over many years.

A number of translations appeared in *Peruvian Rebel, The World of Magda Portal, with a selection of her poems*, Kathleen Weaver © Penn State University Press, University Park, 2009. These are reprinted by permission: "Distant Sea," "Film Vermouth," "Poem," "Song 5," "12 (Alert loneliness)," "13 (Friendship)," "14 (Lens)," "16 (Voluminous white)," "Night," "Bridges," "Pacific Steam," "The Command," "Sailor of Every Sea," "Proletarian Song".

The editors of the following journals are gratefully acknowledged for having welcomed in their pages a number of these translations: *Alcatraz, The Bitter Oleander, Tecalote, Monserrat Review, Exchanges*.

"Film Vermouth" and "18" first appeared in *The Penguin Book of Women Poets*, edited by Carol Cosman, Joan Keefe & Kathleen Weaver.

"Poem," "Proletarian Song," "Film Vermouth," "The Command" and "12" were first drafted by the late Allan Francovich and completed with his encouragement. Sincere gratitude as well to José Garay Boszeta for his editorial guidance, and for his own translations of some of the poems, versions that informed my choices. Above all I am grateful to Bob Baldock, my husband, a critical participant in this and all my efforts.

Magda Portal, Gloria Delmar, Serafín Delmar. México, 1927.

Magda Portal's Other Poetic Voices
by Daniel R. Reedy

Scholars and students are familiar with the committed, political nature of Magda Portal's published works, be they lyric poetry, short story, novel or journalistic essay. As early as 1924, an increasingly strident voice characterized her writings in journals such as *Flechas* and *Trampolín*; in her coauthored volume, *El derecho de matar*, with Serafín Delmar, and ultimately in her collaborations in José Carlos Mariátegui's *Amauta*. By the time of her first forced exile in 1927, she had largely abandoned the Romantic/Modernist voice of her late teens and early twenties and had reshaped her "persona" and poetic voice into a decidedly more radical socialist mode, in keeping with the politically charged concept of vanguardist aesthetics she set forth in her essay, *El Nuevo poema y su orientación hacia una estética económica*, published in 1928.

During the next three decades, voices and actions of other women became models that Magda consciously or unconsciously imitated: Russian socialist and Bolshevik Alexandra Kollontay; Spanish anti-fascist and communist leader Dolores Ibárruri, La Pasionaria; and French-born Flora Tristán Moscoso, a woman of Peruvian parentage, whose action-oriented life and socialist-utopian writings intrigued Magda perhaps more than any other predecessor.

As Magda explored concepts of the woman / writer / political activist / revolutionary that she wished to become, she routinely discarded or suppressed "poetic voices" that burst forth from her inner creative self when they did not seem to fit the prototype she wished to imitate. I include among these Magda's voice as lover, as mother, and as senior woman. In these roles or alternative personae, Magda's cognitive, controlled persona surrenders to a spontaneous self that revels in amorous passion, glories and agonizes in the vicissitudes of motherhood, and searches for comfort and reconciliation in the ruminations of old age. These are voices that Magda could not keep from being born, although she often kept them from being published or from being circulated beyond a small circle of family members and close friends.

In her 1978 interview, "Yo soy Magda Portal", published by Ester Andradi and Ana María Portugal (*Ser mujer en El Perú*), Magda explained that during her exile in Mexico (1927-29) a growing commitment to political activism and the influence of Haya de la Torre led her to destroy her first unpublished book of verse. She says: "Entonces tomé mi libro *Anima Absorta*, y lo rompí íntegro, viendo después como el río arrastraba los pedazos..." (p.214) ["I took my manuscript *Anima Absorta* and ripped it up, then watched the river carry away the scraps."] What she does not reveal is that most of the poems she destroyed had already appeared in *Mundial*, *Mercurio Peruano*, and *Flechas*. As well, she probably had no desire to circulate more widely texts that detailed her amorous relationship with poet Federico Bolaños, the man who fathered her child, the person she later married, and the man from whom she fled in 1925.

In passionate entreaties to her lover, the liberated spirits of Alfonsina Storni and Delmira Agustini resonate in Magda's poems intended for *Anima Absorta* such as "Dónde estabas...?" (1920), "Este momento" (1923), and "Vacío (1926), along with "Vidas de milagro" and "Unete a mí" (1925). In "Vacío", for example, Magda says,

Yo soy tuya y tú eres mío   ¡bésame!
No lloro hoy   Me ahoga la alegría
una extraña alegría
que yo no sé de dónde viene
. . . .
Ven bésame   ¿Qué importa?
Te llamó el corazón toda la noche
Y ahora que estás tú, tu carne y tu alma
¿Qué he de fijarme en lo que has hecho ayer?
          ¡Qué importa!

Ven bésame   tus labios
tus ojos y tus manos
Luego   nada

[I am yours you are mine   kiss me!
I don't weep now   joy floods me
a strange joy
come from I don't know where
. . . .
Come kiss me   What does it matter?
All night my heart called to you
now that you are there, your flesh and blood
why should I think of what you did yesterday
         What does it matter!
Kiss me   your lips
your eyes your hands
Then   nothing]

("Vacío," *Mundial,* 1926)

153

In 1965 when Magda published *Constancia del Ser*, she elected not to reprint poems to her lover and long-time companion Serafín Delmar, even though they figured prominently in the section entitled "el desfile de las miradas" of *Una esperanza y el ma*r (1927). Neither did she select poems from *Costa Sur* (1945) that expressed sentiments of distrust and growing alienation from Serafín during their years of exile in Chile. Customarily, once Magda closed the door on an aspect of her personal life it was as though it had never existed; thus, she expurgated her collected poetry as carefully as Biblical scholars ruled out the apocrypha as unauthentic texts.

Between late 1923 and early 1924, Magda composed eighteen poems, entitled "Vidrios de amor", that recall her pregnancy and the birth of her only child. Gloria, born in November of 1923, was the product of an ill-fated and brutalizing relationship with Federico Bolaños. Magda's plight as an unmarried mother-to-be is the focus of poems addressed to her own mother whose declaration of "vete, nomás" [go, just leave] signaled Magda's expulsion from the Portal Moreno home. For Magda, her mother's fiery silence and alienation are unbearable punishments. Addressing her mother, she pleads,

> carne de mi corazón
> como un pequeño
> te estoy pidiendo abrigo
> calor de tu regazo
> para mis fríos de hoy   de mañana   de siempre
> para mí que una vez
> desconocí tu fuego sacro.

> [flesh of my heart
> like a child
> I ask for your protection
> the heat of your lap
> for the cold I feel today   or tomorrow   or forever
> your sacred fire
> I no longer know.]

("Vidrios de amor", 6)

The painful journey recorded in these poems documents Magda's anguish, complicated by feelings of negativity, self-loathing, and inadequacy in the face of impending motherhood. Gradually, however, the dark side gives way to the tender sentiments of a pregnant woman, the anxieties of a protective mother-to-be, and the will to confront and conquer her personal internal demons.

"Gracia plena", a poem written during her pregnancy, but not published until 1926, offers images of Magda's growing maternal sentiments as her child's birth approaches. The poet says,

¡Cómo tiemblas en mi alma,
cómo tensas mi joven piel rosada,
cómo me agitas toda y tremes, cómo
jadeas en tu encierro de carne deslumbrada!
. . . .
¡Dios mío! Y yo le he dado gota a gota,
la miel del interior de mi colmena,
su celeste sabor llena su boca
toda su carne está en mi alma llena.

[How you tremble in my soul,
my rosy youthful skin becomes taut,
you shake me and make me tremble, how
you gasp in your dazzled cocoon of flesh!
. . . .
My God! And I have given you drop by drop
the interior honey of my hive,
its celestial flavor fills your mouth
all your flesh is cradled in my brimming soul.]

("Poliedro", 1926)

The circumstances of Gloria's birth, Magda's belated marriage, and subsequent divorce from Federico Bolaños were parts of Magda's intimate personal history that she controlled or recrafted. Most of the "Vidrios de amor" were systematically excluded from *Una esperanza y el mar* when it appeared in 1927, except for texts that made no reference whatsoever to pregnancy and motherhood. As well, Gloria bore the surname Delmar, leading the majority of Magda's political associates to believe that Serafín Delmar was the poet's husband and the father of her child.

Magda was a caring, protective, and doting mother, and Gloria travelled with her into exile in Cuba, Mexico and Central America, and later Argentina and Chile. With the exception of a single text, written in the Cárcel de Santo Tomás in 1935, Gloria is never mentioned in Magda's poetry until January 1947, when the young woman commited suicide at age 23. After her daughter's death, Magda's poetic voice as "mother" became her salvation from a nervous collapse that many friends believed would lead her to take her own life. Her poem, "Balada triste", reveals Magda's broken spirit and disorientation in the wake of her daughter's death:

> Todo lo presentía en mí tu ausencia
> la soledad, la quiebra y la derrota
> y esta hora cero sin posibles
> sin mañana ni aurora.
>
> Ya no camino por los años
> detenida en el borde de la vida
> ya no camino   aguardo
> la señal convenida
> en que ataré tus lazos a mis lazos
> e iré a dormir tu noche con la mía.
>
> [Everything makes present your absence
> solitude, collapse and failure
> and this zero hour without possibilities
> with no tomorrow or dawn.

Years don't pass for me
I remain beyond the bounds of life
I do not advance   I await
the agreed upon sign
then I will bind my ties to your ties
and I will fall asleep in your night.]

(*Constancia del Ser*, p.130)

Twenty years after Gloria's death, when I tried to discuss this painful episode with Magda, she responded with anger and weeping. The last lines of "Balada triste" eloquently explain Magda's refusal to share her daughter's memory or the pain of her death with anyone:

No dejo que te rocen las palabras
ni que digan tu nombre ni en voz baja
porque eres sólo mía ahora
mía sin muerte y sin distancia.

[I won't let words even graze you
I won't let your name be pronounced
not even in a low voice
because you belong to me alone now
you are mine without death or distance.]

(p. 131)

Between 1965 and 1988, i.e. from the publication of *Constancia del Ser* to the composition of her last piece, Magda wrote forty additional poems that were to form a volume entitled *Poesía interdicta*. Approximately one-third of the poems appeared in periodicals or were read at public ceremonies. Poems such as "Canto a Cuba", "Himno a Flora Tristán",

"Canto augural a Túpac Amaru", and "Llanto por Nicaragua" are reminiscent of her politically charged poetic rhetoric of earlier decades. The remainder, however, deal with personal themes–memories of the past, solitude, old age, the proximity of death, and mysteries of the Other Side. The initial verses of a poem entitled "Envejecemos", for example, sum up these thematics:

> Envejecemos junto con las cosas
> amamos y dejamos de amar
> > nos cubre el polvo
> > > nos sacude el tiempo
> y olvidamos de ser lo que ayer fuimos

> [We grow old along with the things
> we love and no longer love
> > dust covers us
> > > time shakes us up
> and we forget to be what we were before]

She notes that frailties of old age are revealed by a voice without resonance, an incapacity to recall details of past events, a piece of fruit that looks the same but has a different taste, and spontaneous disconnected memories triggered by an odor or an image from the past.

Some of the poems Magda wrote during her last years have a wry, fatalistic humor in them. "Dudas", written in 1979, captures the poet's awareness of the anxiety her impending death causes her caregiver, her youngest sister Graciela, who wonders with each passing day, "Is this the day when Magda will die?"

> ¡tantas veces he muerto!
> ya no recuerdo cuántas
> . . . .
> ella lo intuye
> > y tiembla

y no poder decirle
       voy a quedarme para siempre
y devolverle el aire
       y el aliento
o tal vez no   tal vez
lo que ella teme es eso
             que no me vaya nunca

[I've died so often!
I can't remember how many times
. . . .
she intuits it
       and trembles
and can't talk about it
       I will remain forever
and give back the air
       and the wind
or perhaps not   perhaps
what she fears is this
             that I will never die]

Poems such as "Seguir aún" (1981) suggest that daily routine in old age is the only proof of existence. Yet there is an awareness that another day of life may not be forthcoming and that only non-existence awaits:

Un día más   de nuevo
tomar el pulso de la sangre
el pan   la ropa   en fin
saber que aún los ojos viran
y las manos perciben
             suaves
cada cosa
. . . .

Tal vez mañana
 Ya no será
  tal vez
    ¿cómo será
    no ser?

[Another day again
take the pulse of its blood
eat get dressed finally
know the eyes are still looking
the hands still touching
   gently
each thing
. . . .
   Perhaps tomorrow
   will not come
    perhaps
      what will it be like
      not to exist?]

Other texts, such as "Estar aquí", are more introspective and philosophical. Written in 1986, it reflects on the circumstances of existence relative to the unknown:

Estoy rodeada de seres extraños, ajenos a mí misma,
nada nos vincula, nuestros caminos son divergentes. No
hay encuentro posible. ¿Cuál es la razón de vivir? ¿para
qué se ama, se procrea, se edifica, se crea de la nada si el
yo magnífico en su identidad es solo miserable momento
de existencia que se extingue junto con la materia que
recubre su pensamiento?

[I am surrounded by strange beings, alien to myself,
nothing connects us, our paths diverge. No encounter
is possible. What is the reason for living? Why does
one love, procreate, build, create out of nothing, if the
I, the self —so magnificent in its identity— is only a
wretched moment to be extinguished along with the matter
that is a garment for its thought?]

At other times, Magda's poetic voice conveys a mental attitude that
is more deeply personal than philosophically reasoned, revealing her
apprehensions when confronted by the proximity of death. In "Quizá
nadie oirá", the lyric voice reflects on the possibility of being entirely alone
when death comes, and no one will hear her last words in the final hour of
life:

Quizá nadie oirá mis últimas palabras
tal vez el mar lejano recogerá mi voz
se juntará la noche con el día y el tiempo
será la noche eternal con su luna de vidrio

[Perhaps no one will hear my final words
perhaps the remote sea will gather in my voice
and night will be one with day and time
eternal night with its glassy moon]

In many of the poems from her posthumous *Poesía interdicta*, there
is an emotional introspection, a process of self-searching, and evidence of
self-analysis that is not characteristic of the vast corpus of Magda Portal's
earlier poetry. As a young author devoted to a vanguardist aesthetic, Magda
endeavored to incorporate Marxist-Leninist tenets into her writings that
demonstrated her commitment to societal change through revolution.
Thus, reader perception has frequently been that Magda's poetry was so

politicized that it was largely devoid of personal emotion. In truth, the public image that Magda wished to project through her writings was that of the "infatigable luchadora" [tireless social fighter], a DNA composite of Alexandra Kollontay, Dolores Ibárruri, and Flora Tristán. Magda's other poetic voices as lover, mother, and senior woman are no less authentic, despite the fact that they are less well known to her readership. In some respects, however, these other voices may be the repositories of Magda Portal's most authentic and enduring poetry.

Daniel R. Reedy
Professor Emeritus of Spanish
University of Kentucky

Magda Portal and her daughter Gloria Delmar. Lima, 1931.

INDEX OF POEMS

Magda Portal & Kathleen Weaver. Berkeley, 1981.

ABOUT THE AUTHOR

Magda Portal (Peru 1900-1989) was not only an acclaimed poet in her early youth but an audacious, free-spirited dissident, increasingly concerned with social justice. Uruguayan writer Eduardo Galeano referred to Portal as "an illustrious and daring rebel," while Salvadoran poet Claribel Alegría affirmed that "not only is Magda Portal an excellent poet, she is an important figure in Latin American history, a feminist voice that reflects the sufferings, needs and hopes of our continent." A key figure in a brilliant Peruvian "vanguard generation" of the 1920s, a group that included the great poet César Vallejo and the Marxist thinker José Carlos Mariátegui, she went on to become a pioneering champion of women's equality, in the context of the larger battle for economic redistribution. Her efforts on behalf of women and the poor may be compared to those of Emma Goldman, Tina Modotti, Rosa Luxemburg, and the French-Peruvian labor leader Flora Tristán. Exiled from Peru in 1927, she was recruited in Mexico City into the revolutionary nationalist APRA movement. When Peru's autocrat Augusto B. Leguía was deposed, she would return with other exiles to Peru to become co-founder and women's leader of the revolutionary nationalist APRA Party of Peru, the American Popular Revolutionary Alliance. She undertook repeated forays into Peru's hinterlands, traveling high into the Andes and deep into the Amazonian jungle, recruiting women, and men, into the first mass political party in Peru's history. As national secretary of women's affairs, she traveled tirelessly, speaking and organizing, often living in clandestinity, and attempting with difficulty to balance the needs of motherhood and of poetry. Her exceptional life was marked by serious hardship, involving imprisonments, exiles, and the ten year jailing of her lover, poet Serafín Delmar. When the APRA party veered to the right in the 1940s, abandoning their radical social agenda, she denounced that party and its leader, her long-time colleague, Víctor Raúl Haya de la Torre. With the rise of the women's movement in the 1970s in Peru, her life's work was embraced by a new generation of activists, and since then her legend has only increased in renown.

ABOUT THE CONTRIBUTORS

Kathleen Weaver is a poet, translator, anthologist of women poets, and biographer. She is author of *Peruvian Rebel, The World of Magda Portal, With a Selection of Her Poems* (Penn State University Press, 2009). She is the co-editor of *The Penguin Book of Women Poets* (Penguin Books, 1978), a landmark anthology of women poets from around the world, where she included the first English translations of Magda Portal's poems. She has translated many Cuban poets, including Fayad Jamís, Roberto Fernández Retamar, Eliseo Diego, Samuel Feijóo, as well as Nancy Morejón's, *Where the Island Sleeps Like a Wing, Selected Poetry* (Black Scholar Press, 1985). She also translated *Fire From the Mountain: The Making of a Sandinista*, by Omar Cabezas (Crown Publishing Group, 1985) and *Nicaraguan Sketches* by Julio Cortázar (W.W. Norton & Co., 1989). A volume of her poetry, *Too Much Happens*, was published by The Post-Apollo Press in 2015. She studied at the University of Edinburgh and at UC Berkeley as a Ford Fellow in Comparative Literature. She lives in Berkeley, California with her husband, Bob Baldock.

Daniel R. Reedy is Professor Emeritus of Spanish in the Department of Hispanic Studies and Dean Emeritus of The Graduate School at the University of Kentucky. His research on aspects of Peruvian Culture developed in 1959 as a Rotary International Fellow in literature and linguistics at the Universidad Nacional Mayor de San Marcos. After completing the Ph.D. (1962) at the University of Illinois with a study of colonial-era satirist Juan del Valle y Caviedes, his professional career began at the University of North Carolina (Chapel Hill), followed by thirty-four years at the University of Kentucky. In 1966-67, a Fulbright Research Fellowship enabled his project on Peruvian vanguard poets in José Carlos Mariátegui's *Revista Amauta*, leading to his growing interest in the poetry of Magda Portal. Several journal articles, book chapters, and papers related to her poetry and essays grew out of the Amauta project. Later, in 1971, the Social Science Research Council sponsored Reedy's return to Peru for extended conversations with Magda. The personal and intellectual relationship that evolved over time was an impetus for Reedy's research, culminating in his comprehensive volume, *Magda Portal, La Pasionaria Peruana. Biografía intelectual* (Lima: Flora Tristán Ediciones, 2000). His efforts over four decades to locate and document the corpus of Magda's poetry produced *Magda Portal. Obra poética completa* (Lima: Fondo de Cultura Económica, 2010). Reedy retired from the University of Kentucky as Professor and Dean Emeritus in 2001. In 2017, he was inducted into The Hall of Fame of the UK College of Arts and Sciences. He is an Honorary Member of The Hispanic Society of America.